What Makes You Laugh?

Pauline Cartwright

Did you smile today?

Did you giggle today?

Did you have a really big laugh today?

It is good to laugh.
It makes us feel good.
It makes us feel happy.
Laughing is fun!

People laugh in different ways.
Some people laugh with a giggle.

Some people laugh
with a snort.

Laughing is good for us.
It helps us stay well.

Most people love to laugh.
Kids can laugh up to 300 times a day!

Some grown ups
only laugh around 15 times a day.
Some don't laugh at all.

Jokes make us laugh.
Here are some jokes.

Q: How do you start a teddy bear race?

A: Ready, teddy, go!

Q: What game do cows love to play at parties?

A: Moosical chairs!

Q: What's grey, has four legs and jumps up and down?

A: An elephant on a trampoline!

Q: What do you get when you cross a kangaroo with a sheep?

A: A woolly jumper!

Animals can make us laugh. They can do funny things.

Some animals seem to laugh, too. Chimpanzees seem to laugh when they are tickled.

Friends can make us laugh.
They can do funny things.

Films can make us laugh.
Cartoons and TV shows
can make us laugh, too.

We laugh at lots of things.
It is good to laugh every day.
But watch out!
It can be hard to stop when you start!